The Country Life

by
Judy Condon

Library of Congress Cataloging-in-Publications Data
The Comfort of Home by Judy Condon
ISBN 978-0-9843332-4-0

Oceanic Graphic Printing, Inc.
105 Main Street
Hackensack, NJ 07601

Printed in China

Layout and Design by Pat Lucas
Edited by Trent Michaels

About the Author

Judy Condon is a native New Englander, which is evident in her decorating style and the type of antiques she collects and sells. Her real passion is 19thC authentic dry red or blue painted pieces. While July's professional career was as a teacher, Principal and Superintendent of Schools in Connecticut, Judy's weekends were spent at her antique shop, Marsh Homestead Country Antiques, located in Litchfield, Connecticut.

When her husband, Jeff, was relocated to Virginia, Judy accepted an early retirement from education and concentrated her energy and passion for antiques into a fulltime business. Judy maintains a website, *http//www.marshhomesteadantiques.com* and has been a Power Seller on eBay® for over eleven years under the name "superct".

With the success of her books and her working relationships with country shops throughout the United States and Canada, Judy created a successful wholesale business featuring hand-poured primitive wax pieces and other handmade country accessories that she sold wholesale to shops. However, time no longer permits Judy to continue that aspect of her business and she now directs her energy into the success of her book series.

Judy has five children and five grandchildren and lives in Spotsylvania, Virginia with her husband Jeff.

Judy's first twelve books in the "simply country" series have been instant hits and most already in their second printing. Judy may be reached through her website, her email address, marshhomestead@comcast.net or by phone at 877-381-6682.

Introduction

As they say in England, "I'm having a clearing out!" I've decided, although I don't like to admit it to my wonderful husband, I have too much stuff. Periodically I wander through our home and identify those items I can part with. As my days become more hectic, I find myself yearning to capture those olden days of country life when "stuff" wasn't a part of the vocabulary. I've also found that while I have grown dependent on my computer, the convenience of large retailers, and the ease of pushing a button to wash dishes, dry clothes, heat and cool our home, and read at night, I long for the days when rooms were sparsely decorated and held only the essentials of simple living.

That is not to say that I want to live the country life scrubbing clothes with lye and baking bread, but I have found that many women my age have reached a point where less is better. I've wondered if modern technology has caused the pace of our lives to quicken so much that our daily lives have become too much of a challenge. As I look around my home and continue to simplify my surroundings, I feel that the elimination of stuff makes my day-to-day living more manageable, as there are fewer things to distract me.

I hear repeatedly from my readers that they too are looking to simplify and down-size. While I suspect that none of us would truly choose to live the country life as it existed in the 18th and 19th centuries, we would agree that we have the best of both worlds. We can appreciate and utilize those modern conveniences we have at our disposal, yet enjoy a slice of the country life through our collections and country decorating.

The "simply country" book series continues to provide us an escape into *"The Country Life"* of the past without the guilt of knowing we have bread to bake or a tub of water waiting to be filled with dirty laundry.

Table of Contents

Chapter 1

❧ ✿ ❧

Robin and Bill Campanale

Who said you can't raise goats in the middle of a city? Robin and Bill Campanale have lived for 28 years in a home built in 1918 in Worcester, Massachusetts, a city of almost 200,000 and yes, they used to raise goats.

I was able to find a parking spot on the side of the busy main street and was delightfully surprised when I stepped through the front door. Many of us are attempting to decorate in a minimalist style; the same cannot be said of Robin. Her many pieces are magnificent.

Robin found a large rotted log in the backyard and tried to make a make-do hornbeam, unfortunately she was unable to ever get it level. Instead of the hornbeam, she converted the log to a planter filled with pansies for the front porch.

Although I visited in early spring, the backyard still proved to be enchanting despite the lack of flowers.

Gary Wirth built the bee skep house in the garden.

The large entryway is a room in itself. Robin's passion is old paint and almost without exception each piece is dry and just right. The red stepback seen at the left side of the photo was purchased from Sue Wirth of Sue Wirth Antiques in Connecticut, one of Robin's favorite dealers. The large red trencher on top is filled with tobacco leaves; throughout her home, Robin places something in each container, most of which she buys at Primitive Thymes in Spencer, Massachusetts.

A small hornbeam displays pheasant feathers on the first shelf. Three tin chamber candlesticks with paint sit atop a small single drawer box with original red paint.

Robin added a faux fireplace beside the cupboard and uses it to display manganese ovoid jugs, treenware, and a bird's nest filled with quail eggs. Bunches of tobacco leaves, fennel, and flax hang from the molding.

The four-slat black chair is early and holds a dough bowl filled with wax corn.

An open top chimney cupboard is a Sally Whims' piece. Early fabric covered books line the top shelf. Bags of flax rest in an early trencher with attic surface on the lower shelf.

A 19thC child's red wagon holds a large sack of sheep wool. Behind it, a tall hornbeam is filled with small brown pods. An early wooden ladle hangs on the side.

Robin dry scraped the jelly cupboard in the corner down to the original blue. The 19thC treenware bowl on top is filled with balls of brown yarn. The early bowl rack holds a remnant of vintage textile.

Gary Wirth built the window shutters behind the sofa in the parlor. A 19thC scrub top tavern table serves as a coffee table. A collection of early hogscrapers, some with original paint, is seen on top. An early red bowl on the table contains a cluster of straw used to make brooms.

A graduated stack of pantry boxes with paint is topped with an early tin lantern.

19thC dry sink with original mustard paint holds a reproduction shelf made by Primitiques. Robin has turned it around to create a cabinet displaying three ovoid jugs.

The child's chair is a make-do. The hanging slant top desk is early and holds a collection of reproduction early newspapers. Gary Wirth made the ratchet candle holder hanging above.

An early green onion bottle is seen on the top shelf of the olive green painted wall cupboard. A large hourglass, a must have in the early 19thC, sits beside two early leather-covered books and a small treen cup on the first shelf.

A mustard and black gameboard holds a large treen bowl on a 19thC two-drawer mule chest in original red paint. A lollipop candle box in blue paint displays clay pipes.

Robin hangs an early mirror with a hogscraper resting on the bottom on the door of a tall chimney cupboard in red paint. The large gathering basket on top is filled with freshly cut bittersweet.

Robin and Bill removed the large posts and transom and installed dowels in the opening between the parlor and the dining room to give the room a cage bar effect.

Robin and Bill's dining room table features a two-board top and holds a large burl bowl filled with dried quince. Over the faux fireplace, an early hooked rug shows a man feeding his horse. An early blanket crane beside it displays a pair of vintage black stockings.

Robin used a Benjamin Moore paint called "Durango" for the trim and moldings.

A large green onion bottle rests on top of the blue gray cupboard in the back corner of the dining room.

Gary Wirth made the small slant top desk on the six-board chest in paint.

A stack of graduated boxes in paint sits on the floor beside a large vintage child's platform toy horse.

Robin bought the large stepback in early red paint from the late Betty Urquhart of The Maynard House. Early painted baskets, mortars, stoneware, painted boxes, and measures fill the shelves.

Robin dry scraped the bench shown above right down to the original blue paint. Unfortunately, she found the top board lacked paint, so she removed it, turned it over and put it back on!

A green onion bottle and two green glass goblets fill the hanging wall shelf in the fourth corner of the dining room. Early pewter with wonderful aged patina rests on the top shelf.

I find the picture upper right breathtaking; it had to be on the front cover! There is so much to see and appreciate that it hardly needs description. Every color of authentic dry paint, it seems, is evident in this photograph.

Each container holds some type of natural drieds.

Robin found her curtains throughout her house at The Seraph in Sturbridge, Massachusetts.

Below the PEAS sign in the corner, a shelf holds mortars and pestles and early jars filled with mustard seed, chamomile, and oregano.

A sawbuck table in blue paint beneath the window displays a sugar cone underneath an early fly catcher; a pitcher of wooden spoons is seen as well as a variety of stoneware jugs.

A large cast iron stove is surrounded by more early painted pieces against a brick wall. With so many beautiful 19thC pieces displayed throughout the kitchen, I asked Robin if she still cooked. She replied that she was "well intended." Bill lamented that they spent $5000 for a stove that is seldom used. (It does fit the décor, though!)

A hanging buttery over the pantry door provides more space for early painted baskets.

Robin has filled the carrier in original green paint seen atop the red jelly cupboard with dried waxed pomegranates.

A small pantry off the kitchen allows Robin to display apothecary chests purchased at Judy Coffey's shop Country Plus in Hopkinton, Massachusetts. Also seen are bowl fillers from Primitive Thymes in Spencer, Massachusetts, zinc lidded early bottles, lanterns, stoneware, and treen.

When Robin began collecting antiques and vintage pieces, she sought old advertising containers. The Keene Mustard box shown on the pantry shelf filled with early rolling pins is one she has kept.

Robin purchased the hanging spoon rack at Louise Villa's The Bowl Barn *in Douglas, Massachusetts.*

The linsey-woolsey blanket on the master bedroom bed is from The Seraph. The bedroom set is not early and Robin didn't hesitate to paint it black to fit the décor in the rest of the house.

The paper-covered boxes on the shelf over the bed are newly handcrafted.

Three small baskets are displayed on an original red wall cupboard beside the bed.

The make-do chair is from The Seraph and was crafted by Primitiques. The candle stand is early and holds a replica of an early tin candle stick.

A four-drawer apothecary hangs in the upstairs hallway over a mustard slant top 19thC desk.

Aprons hang at the end of a claw foot bath tub in the master bath.

Robin found a variety of pond boats, at Michaels a few years ago. The blue carrier holds waxed pomegranates and rests on top of a small 19thC red painted jelly cupboard that Robin uses to store towels.

A TV room upstairs is done primarily in tones of light tans, creams, and whites which accentuate the colors of the early painted pieces.

The mustard cupboard pictured above is used to hold the television. A stack of early 19thC painted firkins with muted tones stands beside it. A small attic surface carrier above holds three ovoid stoneware jugs.

Robin turned a box upright and opened it on the small red table to create a shelf displaying several items, including journals and a clay pipe.

A reproduction mustard wall box hangs next to an open red early cupboard. Early blanket remnants and leather bound books rest on the top shelf.

Robin purchased the early blue painted table and hanging blue wall cupboard from Country Plus in Hopkinton. She also purchased the small book shelf there. Using old boards, Robin made the cant back shelf which holds leather bound books.

Visible from the upstairs hallway looking down, an early chest is filled with gooseneck gourds.

Robin is high-energy, which you might have already guessed. When not caretaking her three grandchildren, she loves woodworking and painting. Needless to say, antiquing is one of her favorite pastimes. On weekends, Robin and Bill enjoy day trips on their cycles.

Although Robin doesn't sell antiques, she does offer consulting in country decorating. She may be reached at 508-798-0483.

Chapter 2

Mary and Adam Spencer

Mary hauled rocks from around the property to create a circular faux well in the front yard.

Many years ago, while on an antique hunt through New Hampshire, I stumbled across a shop in an early house on a side road in the village of Center Ossippee. I was greeted by a woman who mentioned that, in addition to owning a shop, she served fireside dinners to visitors and prepared full meals on the hearth. Her home was spectacular, filled with piece after piece of early 19thC painted furniture and smalls.

Two years ago, I was contacted by Mary Spencer and invited to visit and perhaps photograph the 1785 Cape she and her husband Adam own near Lake Winnipesaukee. I set the date and thought while I was there I would try and locate the home I had discovered years before and perhaps photograph both homes while in the area. I described it at length as best as memory served and after much discussion, learned that Mary was the woman whom I had met years before.

Mary, recently widowed at the time, moved to Center Ossipee from Illinois in September 1998 and completed much of the 1785 home's restoration on her own. As part of her business, Mary held an annual Christmas open house, dressing in costume and serving refreshments typical of the period. In 2005, a graphic designer named Adam Spencer attended one of Mary's Christmas events and asked in advance if she would mind if he appeared in colonial clothing. She replied that she didn't mind but that the other guests might mistake him for an employeee, as Mary's assistants also dressed in period clothing. After the open house, not a word was heard from Adam until the following Christmas, when Adam appeared at the 2006 open house and spent the entire day. A week later, on a Sunday, Adam appeared standing at Mary's door with an armload of grocery store flowers (all he could find on a Sunday) and asked if he could court her in 18thC style–and he didn't care how long it took. Adam and Mary were married two years later in a 200 year-old New Hampshire barn decorated in a forest woodlands theme. The contra dance reception with fiddlers, line dancing, and the Virginia Reel was attended by fifty guests. Since then Mary and Adam have worked together to transform their 18thC Cape into a first period home furnished with many authentic 17th and 18thC pieces.

Mary and Adam cut down saplings and birch trees which they bend and use as a trellis to hold their climbing clematis.

The front door used to have windows on either side which were not original to the house. Mary and Adam opted to remove the windows and replace them with solid cedar boards. Using the pattern from an early 17thC door, Mary measured and traced the lines on the boards while Adam hammered a reproduction rose head nail at each intersection of lines to create the diamond pattern. The wooden latch is attached to a rope which is threaded through the door, again typical of the 17thC style. When the rope is pulled, the wooden bar is hoisted. The expression "raising the bar" was derived from this English style of construction.

Mary and Adam converted Mary's shop into a 17thC Tap or Tavern Room. Adam built the cage bar, the focal point in the room.

The sawbuck tavern table with scrub top and black base is late 18thC.

Adam painted the Spencer's Ordinary sign as a gift to Mary. The sign is patterned after the 250 year-old Westerwald jug sitting on the mantel beneath it.

Both the Cromwellian black side chairs and the upholstered chair date to the 17thC. Some of Adam's authentic 17thC reenactment clothing hangs from pegs beside two strap sacks, which were also called "possibility bags"; the sack would hold everything a hunter could possibly need. Adam made the hanging candle holder. Every lantern and lighting device in the Spencer home is authentic and has been electrified by Adam over the years. The onion bottle is early.

A small buttery is tucked in the corner. Mary and Adam are determined that everything in the house have meaning. The hanging iron cow feeder holds the shells of organic eggs. When Mary first moved to New Hampshire, a neighbor would bring Mary goose eggs with shells of lovely colors. Mary would blow out the eggs and save the shells which she stores in the feeder.

The bee skep was found in New Hampshire and rests on a shelf made of 18thC barn board, also from New Hampshire.

The bar hanging on the wall, seen in both pictures, holds a rough stone. Mary returned home one day to find the stone placed on her front steps with a note from a neighbor, who had found the stone while cleaning out an old barn and thought Mary would like it. They believe it is an early scouring rock used for scrubbing clothes.

The hand-hewn wooden sink is 17thC and features a small drain made from a hollowed out branch in place of a pipe. The homemade soap was a gift from a friend. The cornhusk broom was made by Jerri Cossett of Kentucky Roots and was a wedding gift to Adam and Mary.

Adam and Mary do all their remodeling. They removed four vinyl floors and two subfloors in the kitchen before putting down a new oak plank "floating" floor.

The counters are soapstone. Adam and Mary had a soapstone sink made and then sanded the front to give it an aged look.

The kitchen shelf is made from 250 year-old planks given to Adam and Mary by a friend. The shelf holds a collection of early treen and a porcelain Bellermine jug. The jug is named after St. Bellermine of Germany and features a relief of a bearded man as its distinguishing characteristic.

The lantern seen right is one of three period lanterns in the kitchen. Mary and Adam have electrified all their period lighting pieces and use only period lighting throughout the house.

Adam made the wall table with a single leg and shoe foot base, which fits tightly against the wall when not in use.

The dining room table is 17thC and matches almost perfectly with the 17thC matched set of original chairs from England. The hanging brass chandelier is a 1950's copy of a 17thC Hapsburg Double Eagle chandelier.

The six-board chest is one of Adam and Mary's favorite pieces as it has descended in an unbroken line through Adam's family. Made in Rowley, Massachusetts, it is signed 1678 and initialed JB.

Sitting on top is a small Bible Box with detailed carving, circa 1680.

The cage is actually a livery cupboard dating to the 1630's and identical to one shown in a book by John Fiske on early antiques. The cupboard was used to store food such as bread and cheese for light meals. Hanging on the left is an initialed PF antique grain sack.

Drieds hang over an early 19thC chest which closely resembles a 17thC piece. It is paneled with grain painting and was purchased at Nashville.

A Bellermine jug rests beside a 17thC English spice box. The spice box features small drawers, each with its original teardrop pull.

A spoon rack with a tombstone heading holds early pewter spoons. The Wainscot armchair, also referred to as a "great chair" for a man only, is early 17thC. Mary made the linsey-woolsey chair pad.

The large table shown below is perhaps American and dates to the late 1600's or early 1700's. The table still features its original chamfered stretcher base legs.

The table is set with early redware plates and pewter utensils.

The chairs are covered with leather and have embossed leather backs.

In the corner, a court cupboard would have been used to store linens. It is elegantly designed with cup and cover turnings. Sitting on top is a newly-crafted book holder which fits the 17thC décor beautifully. Adam electrified the candles behind it.

Adam hand carved a horn cup, similar to the one seen beside the Bellermine jug, for each of his four groomsmen; each cup featured the wedding date and the initials "aSm".

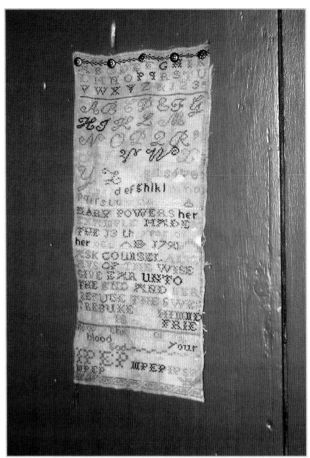

One of Adam's 17th wool coats, used during reenactments, hangs on the door leading to the front entrance.

The sampler wrought by Mary Powers, dated 1790, hides the thermostat.

The fishing pole hanging over the door was unearthed from old masonry when Mary rebuilt the fireplace. It was found tucked behind the wall and still retains the original string.

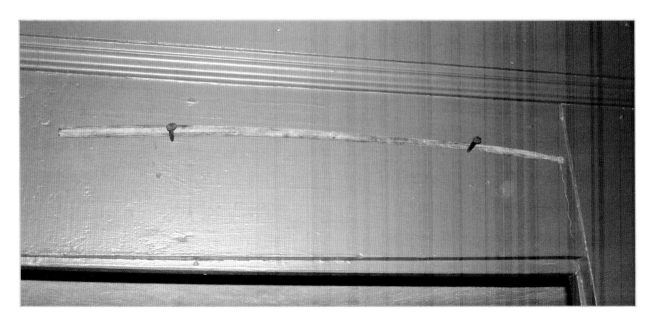

Adam and Mary found the bed initialed "TMA" in Williamsburg. They had seen only one or two of these beds ever before, and, while shipping from Virginia proved to be a chore, they both knew they couldn't turn it down. The bed is dated 1686 and purportedly belonged to Ken Farmer from the "Antiques Road Show".

The carved coffer in front of the windows was found in Maine and covered with shiny varnish. Mary scrubbed the piece with de-natured alcohol to remove the shine.

Resting on top of the chest, a 17thC Bible Box with provenance was purchased from a dealer in Massachusetts, who Mary suspects didn't realize what was inside. Mary discovered a handwritten note within, which revealed that the box, circa 1672, had been a gift from cathedral workers to the Bishop of Durham, England. When King Charles was executed and the bishop banished to France, he was able to escape with the Bible Box.

The chair shown to the left of the mantel features a carved back panel and dates to the 17thC. It rests beneath a framed early mirror surrounded by stumpwork embroidery.

Adam built the shelf in the corner of the "borning room". Mary made the window treatments with authentic linsey-woolsey cloth.

The 18thC carved chest is a copy of a 17thC centennial piece. The braces are patterned after miniature court cups. It would have been used to hold linens or documents.

An early wig stand rests on the top shelf. The hanging clothing conceals a flat screen television!

Mary operates her shop, The Country Lady Antiques, *from their home located at 39 Rt. 16B in Center Ossipee, New Hampshire. Please contact Mary and Adam through their website, www.countryladyantiques.com or by phone: 603-539-5099.*

Chapter 3

Kathy Spellacy

Some readers may recognize the name Spellacy from one of my previous books, as Kathy's parents' Cape Cod home was featured in The Warmth of Home. Kathy lives in York, Maine in a 1972 cape surrounded by 500 acres of woodland held in a land trust and a stone's throw from the ocean. Kathy moved to Maine from South Carolina and immediately began work on the house by tearing out shrubs, replacing the roof, and planting flower beds. Kathy says she has collected antiques since she was five years old; she started by collecting oil lamps and tobacco tins and remembers visits to Brimfield with her mother, who would give her a dollar or two and allow her to wander no more than two aisles away.

The large tin daisy on the front door gives the entire house a welcoming and whimsical look.

Kathy uses tones of creams, whites, and other soft colors throughout her home, accenting with early painted smalls. A single board top scrub table with red paint serves as a coffee table. An early hooked rug remnant is draped on top.

Early baskets, each with rich patina, fill the bench Kathy has creatively hung on the wall.

Kathy found the narrow chimney cupboard in New Hampshire. The rocker beside it is early 18thC and one which Kathy uses when she knits. A chalky trencher hangs on the wall above the chair.

Kathy collects make-dos and the cant back shelf on the scrub top table is filled with them. A small white step stool sits on the floor below it.

Two six board chests in dry red paint hold a large glass jar holding stone fruit, a Christmas present from her mom. A doll chair in paint featuring acorn finials can be seen at the edge of the picture. Kathy has filled the wall shelf with sewing spools, old fabrics, and rag balls, displaying her passion for textiles, vintage sewing pieces, and rug hooking. Kathy owns a wool shop, Woolen Goods, in Rollinsford, New Hampshire, and conducts retreats and classes two or three times a year.

Kathy is particularly proud of four Shaker pin cushions shown in the right hand corner.

Above the early maple candle stand with red paint, a sewing pocket displays threads and bobbins. The old scissors creates an interesting pattern against the wall. The wonderful chalky white candle stand is a reproduction that blends beautifully with Kathy's other pieces.

Kathy couldn't resist the white bench even though she calls the paint "junky." It allows a dimensional display of children's shoes, baskets, and a small child's chair. A knitting pocket on the wall holds needles.

Kathy's kitchen is done in soft greens. The hanging cupboard shown left came from a 1780 farmhouse and is missing its back or top. Kathy used green lattice as a backdrop on the early three board top green table. The metal mat on the wall features a series of small hearts, which makes it a sought after item by collectors.

Kathy found the pie safe with original hearts and stars at York Antique Gallery. The large bucket on the right side is a lidded kerosene bucket. A standing Betty Lamp is tucked behind a green cheese bucket and an early firkin.

The small cubby on the counter is a reproduction and was a housewarming gift. Dried corn cobs are displayed on a vintage corn dryer and hang from a peg board with porcelain knobs.

Kathy ripped out a cupboard and in its place built the wall shelves using old boards found beneath a church; the shelves display tin lidded jars and treen.

A collection of vintage laundry forks and whisk brooms hangs on the wall in the laundry area off the kitchen.

Kathy found three old painted boards in Maine which her Dad used to build the dining room table; he painted the legs to match the tabletop.

Early pewter plates are displayed in a reproduction wall rack. Below, a handmade oval wallpaper box sits on an early high bench.

Kathy treasures the set of three huge ironstone bowls found in the corner cupboard. She has filled the bottom bowl with early blue and white rag balls.

In the back corner, early wooden signs surround a wall shelf with a collection of vintage children's shoes.

Kathy continues the tones of whites and creams in the first floor bathroom. The mirror over the sink was made from an old chalky white cathedral window frame. An early grungy white carrier sits atop a white cupboard over the commode.

An early white bucket serves as a waste basket. Kathy adds texture to the room by hanging a vintage christening dress beside the shower.

Kathy made the hooked rug from a pattern she purchased at The Woolley Fox in Pennsylvania.

The 19thC cupboard with salmon paint sits on a feed trough with wide board top which Kathy's father added. Kathy's father also made the small blue wall cupboard with a salmon paint interior to match the jelly cupboard. Kathy couldn't resist the scalloped edge on the small desk which she uses as a bed table.

Kathy's collection of vintage change purses leans against a chalky white carrier on top of the four draw bureau.

Children's vintage clothing hangs on a peg rack in the guestroom. The soft painted green mule chest is a New England piece.

Kathy was drawn to the surveyors stand because of its early authentic paint. It takes up little space in the corner and is ideal for holding a plant. I actually have one as well which I use in my garden to display a birdhouse.

The upstairs bathroom uses many of the same colors as the first floor bathroom. A framed starfish adds a Cape Cod touch.

The third bedroom features a vintage
collection of sewing utensils, early thread,
and textiles; Kathy uses the room as a
sewing room. The top shelf holds a can of
old rulers and a pair of velvet pin cushions.
The middle shelf holds a Shaker pin
cushion. A vintage spool holder in green
paint rests on the corner of the white table.

Early tin lidded jars hold vintage pin
cushions, threads and buttons. Some of
Kathy's wool from her shop stands ready to
be cut and used for hooking.

A small wall cupboard holds early hat pins, quilting pins, and pin cushions while another shelf displays more of Kathy's make-dos.

Kathy admits that her work as a U.S. Marshall hunting fugitives provides a living but is not who she is. Her home reflects her passions: rug hooking, knitting, punch needlework, cross stitching, and antiquing.

Kathy recently purchased a full line of Patsy Becker rug hooking patterns for the shop. She invites nationally known teachers to conduct workshops throughout the year. For information on Kathy's shop Woolen Goods, please call 603-834-6587 or access her website at www.woolengoods.com.

Chapter 4

Molly and Scott Garland

Molly and Scott purchased their 1746 home in Douglas, Massachusetts from an elderly couple who lived without running water and electricity. An outhouse in the back was still in use when Scott and Molly took possession of the house.

The house was one of three homes belonging to the Chase family in a small village called Tinker Town, as most of the men were tinsmiths. In fact, a small brook running behind Scott and Molly's house is called Tinkers Brook.

When Scott and Molly moved in they immediately added a bathroom and created a kitchen from the attached carriage shed. The door now leading into the house was originally in the kitchen. An early grinding wheel can be seen outside the door to the small addition that Scott and Molly added off the kitchen.

Molly and Scott used "Hadley Red" from the Benjamin Moore historical collection on their cupboards and walls. Molly's father, Gary Wirth, used a scrub top table top to build the make-do kitchen table. An early dough bowl holds fresh onions and potatoes. The Windsor thumb back chairs are early.

Molly and Scott have occasionally helped an elderly woman, who in appreciation gifted to them the long apothecary shown on the kitchen counter. It features original dove tailed drawers and holds a collection of bread boards.

Tucked in the corner, a collection of stoneware jugs and crocks is nestled amidst early tin lidded glass jars and a measure filled with small pomegranates.

Molly's father whittled the candlestick holder from an old stump. Molly alternates using it either as a candle holder or a candle dryer.

An early hanging cupboard in original surface holds an array of butter presses and treen sugar bowls.

A paint decorated Windsor child's chair shows wonderful wear on the arms and footrest.

The small early 19thC jelly cupboard with red paint stands just inside the door and holds a black painted box with dinner napkins. A large dough board provides a backdrop.

A 19thC two door large cupboard has been scrapped down to the original mustard over red paint. An early butter churn stands on the floor beside it.

Molly used a Benjamin Moore paint called "Buttered Yam" on the trim in her dining area, which used to be the tavern area. An 18thC stretcher base table with original red painted surface sits in the middle of the room surrounded by a red painted arm chair and black ladder back.

A small carrier has been mounted on the wall as a display shelf holding pewter mugs, leather bound books, and early textiles.

Tucked under the window, a six board chest dates to the 18thC and retains all of its bittersweet paint.

Angled in the corner, an 18thC cupboard holds glassware. A collection of stoneware jugs and crocks are displayed on top. Molly's father made the spoon rack.

Molly has placed an old barrel lid on the wall above the large gray barrel she uses for storage. A bucket bench displays early painted dough bowls. Molly purchased a collection of stuffed roosters to display at a show in Massachusetts before learning that she wasn't allowed to sell them. She refers to the one shown below, the last of the collection, as her "mascot."

The large standing corner cupboard is actually an early slaughtering bin with original bittersweet paint which Molly and Scott found in Pennsylvania. The deep shelves are ideal for showing off some of Molly's basket collection. A small wooden child's chair hangs beside it.

Molly and Scott rescued the apple green cupboard shown left, from the chopping block. It is an early Connecticut River valley piece which Molly scrubbed down to a more mellow apple green color.

The 18thC green painted table in the center of the living room was found in Rhode Island. The early burl bowl is filled with stone fruit. The Shaker ladder back chair in bittersweet paint is circa 1830 and was found on Cape Cod.

Next to a pale colored wing back chair, an early 18thC New England candle stand features traces of mustard paint. The pine wall box above is constructed with hand-cut screws dating the box to the early 19thC.

The sage green corner cupboard with red paint holds a collection of early pewter. This cupboard is my favorite piece in the house.

Molly and Scott have placed a canted lift top desk on the wall above the 19thC settle in black paint; they use the desk to display leather bound books and early bottles. The small watercolor is marked on the back, "Stone Castle in Warwick Rhode Island 1875". The small globe is a vintage piece which has been in Scott's family for years.

The room features the paint shown when Scott and Molly purchased the home; the color is a perfect match for the soft green tones of the pewter cupboard. A small hooked mat further enhances the cupboard's sage green and red tones.

An early cupboard with mustard paint hangs just inside the front door and above a ladder back with acorn finials.

Scott collects books pertaining to the Civil War and also inherited many Zane Grey books from his father. A large wall shelf displays his book collection surrounding an early single drawer pine desk.

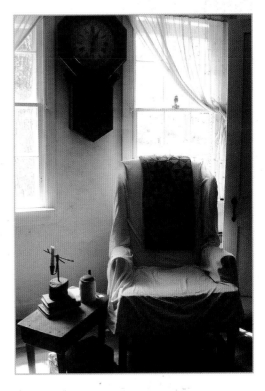

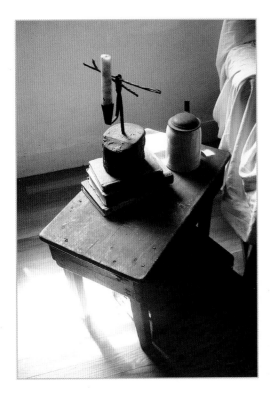

A glass display case holds some of Scott's early rock and shell collection.

Scott also likes to collect early bottles and has unearthed many on his property.

An early school clock hangs on the wall between the windows. An 18thC rush light rests on a stack of early books on the small table beside the upholstered chair.

Molly operates her shop, Tinker Town Antiques, in a small barn behind their house. She is open by chance or appointment and on Fridays 10-1. Molly also sells in the Sturbridge Antique Shop on Rt. 20 in Sturbridge, Massachusetts.

Molly enjoys working with her mother, Sue Wirth, who has been an antique dealer for a number of years. Sue and Molly work together at the Brimfield Show, the Nan Gurley Show in November in Marlboro, Massachusetts, and the Sutton Massachusetts Antique Show in September. Scott, a former fire chief, now sells fire equipment and participates in the antique business since his retirement from the fire department three years ago.

Molly may be reached via email at mollygarland@gmail.com or by phone 508-476-5193.

Chapter 5

Colette Donovan

Colette Donovan lives in a small river village in Massachusetts that she refers to as, "A place time forgot." There are no homes built later than 1860 and each home has a history of its own. Colette has been an antique collector and dealer for over twenty-five years and specializes in 18thC early American country pieces and related textiles.

When Colette and her husband Jim purchased their dream home in 1996, much of the restoration had been completed. Still, they called in Richard Irons, the guru of early chimney restoration in the northeast. After examining the original firebox which supports all the fireplaces and the brick archways in the basement, he corrected the original date of the home to be late 17thC as opposed to the 1729 date given by previous owners.

After meeting Colette and spending time with her in person and later by phone, I began to feel that I could guess why a particular piece in her home appealed to her. Colette has a whimsical side that reveals itself in her selection of pieces which are, to use her words, "not normal." While most of us have treasures with a story, Colette's keen eye looks for the authentic piece with a unique quality about it ... the "soulful survivors."

Entering by the side door, a visitor first encounters a Queen Anne chest in dry green paint dating to 1720. Resting on top, a miniature chest in green paint still retains its original till. An early watering can in green paint can be seen at the edge of the picture. The early drying basket on the wall would have been used for drying flowers or herbs.

A pair of early 18thC protective shoes called pattens is one of Colette's unique pieces. The leather has been treated with a tar and oil mixture to protect them from the mud on wet days.

The 9' open hearth was the most compelling reason to purchase this old house. It retains its original firebox.

Hanging to the left of the fireplace, a homespun blanket drapes over a blanket crane to conceal a recess that the previous owner built to provide a hose in case of fire.

The rocking chair shows its original red surface and seat woven from the bark of a tree.

Colette pointed out the missing bricks in the back of the fireplace. The ingenious 17thC design acts as an exhaust system to direct the smoke up the chimney.

A demi-lune punched tin plate warmer is surrounded by stone fruit on the mantel.

Colette placed an 18thC fish broiler at the opposite end of the mantel to balance the grater, part of the Corbin iron collection. It rests above an early sunflower patterned pot holder. An early hand-carved quail sits on a perch beside a container of fresh wildflowers. Colette has a passion for birds and baskets, both tastefully exhibited throughout the house.

Hanging on the edge of the mantel is a rare beam duster. The end of the long handle shows wear, indicating that perhaps it was used by a small child whose chore was to remove the spider webs from the ceiling.

Just visible on the inside edge of the fireplace is a treen funnel. A shot pouch and powder horn hang beside it.

An unusual 18thC hatchel in the shape of a whale hangs above the homespun blanket to the left of the mantel. The split in the wood almost gives the whale a warm expression.

Colette purchased the hobby horse resting on the Massachusetts North Shore pewter cupboard because she thought its head gave it somewhat of "an attitude." The hobby horse reinforces Colette's passion and awe about our forebearers who accomplished so much without benefit of modern advantages. A collection of treen, including a very early American chestnut strainer and an American chestnut mortar and pestle can be seen above.

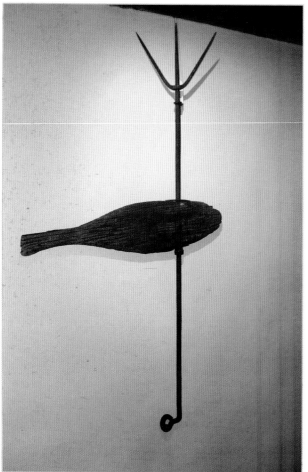

An early sawbuck table in dry gray paint is surrounded by ladder back chairs in black. A 17thC American chestnut slab bench is barely visible on the left side of the picture. A hand turned 18thC salmon painted burl bowl rests in the center of the table.

In a place of honor on a hallway wall, the 18thC fish weathervane is mounted on its original iron holder ending in a lightning rod. The worn wood exhibits a magnificent patina.

Tucked under the window, a large simple 19thC gathering basket sits on top of a first period early 18thC storage bin with shoe feet and wooden dowel hinges. It measures a full 74" long and retains its original knobs and attic surface.

The 18thC desk seen right is called an apothecary desk and was probably used in a country store. It features original butterfly hinges. The basket on top conceals a sound system speaker. An 18thC iron rooster weathervane in original surface stands beside a half round 19thC hooked rug.

A cookie mold hangs on the wall behind the rooster.

A previous owner, when restoring the house in the 1970's, researched the windows and commissioned the custom-made leaded glass windows for the Keeping Room.

The large table and chairs in the dining room are the only remaining reproductions in the house, and Colette is anxious to replace them. But with her need to seat twelve, she still has an antique table on her list!

Shown below left, the New England chest with high scalloped base is probably from southern New Hampshire. There is no hardware nor was there ever because oftentimes the first owner was too poor to afford imported brass. What makes the chest special is that no one ever drilled holes for knobs. The wear on the sides of the drawers is almost grooved and gives evidence of how the drawers open. A child's chair made from a log is visible beside it. The hanging gourds come from the collection of the late and highly-respected New Hampshire antique dealer Roger Bacon.

The William and Mary gothic style andirons are from Europe. This fireplace in the dining room features remnants of the original parging, a mixture of sand and bonding agent smeared over the bricks to protect them.

The 17thC settle chair in brown paint is the first antique Colette ever purchased. An 18thC fragment of American crewel embroidery hangs above. Each flower was cut from the tattered original linen and reapplied in the 19thC.

The mirrored sconce retains its original glass with a replaced candle cup.

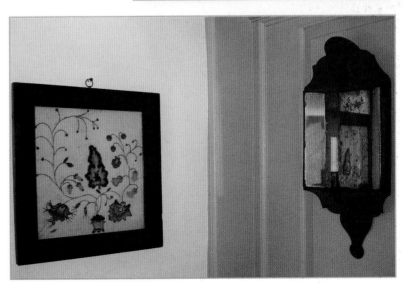

The living room raised paneling is painted a restful shade of pale gray. The color was chosen to reflect the angled views of the Merrimac River visible from the front windows.

As mentioned earlier, Colette appreciates the unusual; the candle stand on the hearth in her living room is a perfect example. A large piece of burl replaces what was most likely legs at one time. The early New England armchair beside it is also unique in that the arms are slanted with early mushroom hands and finials. It is an early New England piece.

Seen beside the doorway to the front entrance, an early 19thC tall clock with original red paint features a delightful saw tooth base. The clock face is adorned with a painting of the famous Portland Light in Maine.

In the front hall opposite the clock, an 18thC demi lune table with original dry surface holds a primitive chalky white shorebird and nest.

Colette once sold an expensive piece to a client and allowed the client to pay over a lengthy period of time. In gratitude, the client presented Colette with a book entitled The Ladies Worktable which included the collections of Professor and Mrs. Miller's needlework in which the horse rug on the wall was pictured.

The rare, 18thC single- drawer chest below is smoke grained, a process of moving a lighted candle to and fro to create patterns as the paint begins to cure. An 18thC turned maple dough bowl with remnants of original green paint sits on top.

Behind the couch, a six-board chest in pale green holds a late 18thC or early 19thC horse in chalky white that shows much use and love. Colette was drawn to the piece by its stand up mane and remains of a horsehair tail.

Between the front windows, an 18thC chest, cleaned down to its original blue-gray fits perfectly under the molding. A carved folk art toy horse has long since lost its mane, attached at one time with rose head nails.

The portrait of a woman with lovely lace and a dress with perfect color for the room hangs above a desk; Colette gave the desk to her husband at Christmas as a thank-you for his constant support for her and her antique business. The original green ladder back chair dates to the 18thC and was purchased because the back is warped.

A single drawer blanket chest in original dry attic surface is an ideal fit for the corner in the master bedroom. The gunstock corners at the back of the house are original and never painted. It was common to leave the beams in the back rooms undressed, while the beams and gunstock corners in the front of the house were encased and painted.

The six-board gray chest holds a basket of towels. To Colette's thinking, one can never have enough old baskets; she uses them in each room of the house. An early needlework hangs on the wall and provides a perch for a folk art carved songbird and its nest.

The armchair shown right is an early indigo blue make-do chair upholstered in indigo linen. The octagonal table beside it holds a 17thC Bible which Colette treasures. It has areas on the front leather cover which are totally worn through from use. An unusual very early thumb candle holder stands beside the book. The pair of tulip-shaped tin sconces on the wall lights an early watercolor of a schoolgirl.

An early tall bureau with a lollipop drop in the middle and no hardware shows worn edges on the drawers from use.

An early miniature six-board chest with a beautiful scalloped base sits on the bureau.

After seeing the potato stamped walls of the Boardman House, an historical building at the Saugus Iron Works, Colette decorated her guest bath walls with a potato dipped in a Spanish brown paint.

Double and twin beds, found in a horse barn, provide sleeping room when her children come to visit. The chestnut stand with chamfered top and simple pedestal was once owned by Roger Bacon.

Beside the rocking chair, an interesting early scalloped table top features an engraved floral pattern.

Shown to the left, a Pilgrim period chest with a single drawer and old paint holds a Connecticut floral painted decorated dome top box dating to the 18thC. The mirror's frame dates to the 18thC, but the looking glass has been replaced.

On the stairwell, Colette has placed an unusual dressed heddle, meaning someone painstakingly placed the threads on the loom to represent a large amount of work. This is the stage prior to weaving with the weft. Colette's passion for 18thC textiles, coupled with her eye for artistic quality and appreciation for the work required to dress the loom, made the dressed heddle a keeper.

Colette's porch overlooks a lovely backyard bordered by vinca and evergreens.

The unusual cedar root was found in a pile at the back of the yard. It has a place of honor supporting ivy outside the Keeping Room window.

Colette purchased the early rocker in blue paint because of its oversized rockers. It's quite a conversation piece and brings smiles to the faces of many guests.

The name of Colette's business is Colette Donovan. She is a member of The Antique Dealers Association of America and exhibits at many fine national shows. She is available by appointment only and may be reached at 978-346-0614.

Chapter 6

✦ ✳ ✦

Shelly Leclaire

Shelly Leclaire of Milford, Massachusetts decided six years ago to convert her single 1993 home into a duplex and rent the other side. The result is a charming natural shingled home with the charm of a quaint cottage. A visitor soon realizes that the interior is considerably larger than it appears from the outside.

Shelly has been working diligently to create a country garden in the back of her home. Unfortunately, the masses of perennials she planted had not yet bloomed when I visited during early spring.

Stone paths meander through flower beds to a potting shed in the back corner of the yard. Shelly uses forms constructed with natural twigs and branches as a trellis for her climbing plants.

She contracted a local carpenter to create cupboards resembling the Shaker form. The finish is a specially mixed paint with an antiqued glaze to give the cupboards an aged appearance. Shelly uses the tips of wooden clothespins as knobs.

Shelly widened the windowsill over the sink to allow for additional display space for her collections. Graduated dough bowls rest on either side of an early dough box.

Shelly is in the process of collecting early dough boards to cover the Corian countertops. She finds that the Corian requires too much upkeep for her lifestyle and doesn't quite blend with the aged appearance she was hoping to achieve in the kitchen.

A spectacular Shaker bucket with a traditional diamond bracket and original blue paint is filled with cinnamon sticks. Italian fruit bread known as panettone rests in an early wooden scoop. Shelly purchased the hanging spoon rack from Country Plus in Hopkinton, Massachusetts.

A miniature mortar and pestle sits on a breadboard next to a collection of Majolica pitchers. The large yellow ware batter bowl in mint condition was also purchased at Country Plus.

Shelly's mother painted the primitive scene on a breadboard leaning behind miniature fly screens. Shelly turned an early wooden box upside down, creating a platform to display stoneware crocks and small treen.

A stack of early red benches sits on the floor beneath a peg rack holding bunches of Sweet Annie and treen. Shelly mounted a breadboard and Sweet Annie on the end of the overhead cupboards.

Shelly purchased both the 19thC horse with chalky white paint and hanging corner cupboard in red paint at Country Plus. The floor cloth was painted by Sue Rice, former owner of Antiques on the Common in Grafton, Massachusetts.

A bookrack with leather strap and an early book rests atop an early desk in red paint under the front window.

Shelly's dining room area is an extension of the kitchen work area. Early cupboards in paint and a variety of treen with country colored paint are tied together with the diamond-patterned floorcloth made by Sue Rice. Shelly has placed two breadboards on top of the 19thC dry sink to give the top a graduated height. A small four-drawer box rests at one end beneath an early fly screen. A large out of round dough bowl is overturned at the other end and fills the well. On the scrub top table with black base, the canted dough box holds a collection of oval bowls. The chairs, purchased at Country Plus, are reproduction pieces.

The early cupboard with salmon paint fits perfectly under the window; it holds a dry painted gray carrier filled with trenchers.

A graduated set of berry baskets is displayed with treenware on the primitive shelf above the sink.

On the opposite wall, a 19thC mustard stepback provides ample room to show off some of Shelly's carrier collection.

A weathered old ladder holds a gooseneck gourd and Sweet Annie. The stack of chests in paint on the floor rests beside a large butter churn beneath a shelf holding manganese pottery, a sieve, and an oval bowl.

Shelly uses an old door featuring original hardware tucked in the corner as the means to display a replica of an early American flag.

A 19thC large measure in blue paint rests atop a tall chimney cupboard in the corner. Shelly has inverted an early breadboard with terrific patina and displays it on the wall over a chalk white bench with bootjack ends.

This picture below, taken from the stairway provides another view of the living room. The natural wood tone of the pine floors that Shelly put down gives the entire house a sense of openness. The double raised panel door cupboard is 19thC and shows wonderful wear. Above it hangs a cupboard in cobalt blue early paint; having lost its door long ago, the cupboard thus provides additional display for more of Shelly's textiles and treen. The small blue cupboard is a reproduction.

In the corner behind the couch, which I understand has been replaced with a camel back sofa since my visit, a two-door cupboard with raised panels hangs above a narrow drop leaf table with red paint. A lollipop-handled candle box in mustard rests on top of the cupboard.

The wall shelf holding small cutting boards is a reproduction; the candle box in attic surface hanging below is early. Shelly placed the box on the wall to conceal her doorbell chime.

The corner chair on the stairway landing is old. The corner cupboard above it holds more of Shelly's majolica pitcher collection.

I hear repeatedly that my books provide great ideas to others, and Shelly's creative window treatment in the downstairs bathroom is one such example. Shelly cut an old dough board with breadboard ends in half to make window shutters.

A handcrafted mirror with shutters, purchased at Brown and Hopkins in Rhode Island, hangs over the vanity. The copper sink is actually Shelly's great-grandmother's pot, which she used to cook polenta. According to Shelly, polenta, also known as poor man's food, is made from hardened corn meal.

Shelly placed an early lap desk with original surface over the commode.

Shelly started collecting by going to yard sales and flea markets, and, as expected, her tastes have evolved over the years from oak pieces and reproductions to authentic early antiques.

In one year, Shelly has replaced almost every piece on the first floor and is now working on renovating the bedrooms. She says it has been an expensive growth experience but doesn't regret what it has taken to achieve the home she has and always wanted. When not working for the town of Milford, Shelly enjoys visiting her favorite spots: Country Plus *in Hopkinton,* The Barn Bowl *in Douglas, and* Red House Primitives *in Holliston, Massachusetts.*

Chapter 7

❖ ⊛ ❖

Marjorie and Al Staufer

Marjorie and Al live in central Ohio in a home that they moved board by board from Plympton, Massachusetts. The house was built circa 1690-1700 by Isaac King, who was born in 1640. When Al and Marge received a call from an antique dealer friend telling them about the house, they quickly drove to Brookfield, Massachusetts and, seeing nothing more than a standing frame and a pile of beams and boards, made the decision to purchase the structure. They had the house reconstructed in 1976 on 75 acres they owned across the street from their 1830 Greek Revival home in Ohio.

Al, a retired art teacher who has written ten books on eastern railroads, keeps a 22' X 50' "O" gauge model train layout in their barn. Marge has been a dealer of fine antiques for over 40 years and is highly respected for her expertise. Many of her pieces have been noted in some of the homes I photographed for previous books in the "simply country" series.

An early sundial, most likely of English origin, dates to the early 18thC and reads "amongst ye floures, ye count thee houres".

In preparation for the reconstruction of their house, Marge purchased early hardware, an example of which is found on the back door. This door knocker dates to the 18thC.

Entering from the side door, a visitor steps into the buttery built with extra boards from an 1810 addition to the original house. The buttery is a copy of the one in the Tristram Coffin house in Newbury, Massachusetts, and is filled with treasures. Marge waited patiently to unwrap these treasures when the house was finally finished and said it felt like Christmas.

Marge particularly likes the simple lines of the New England dry sink in original paint. The rich blue paint and deep backsplash make it unique. It dates to the 1820's. Notice the gorgeous dry blue painted apple basket found in Vermont hanging above.

Marge tries to purchase all the furniture in the house from Massachusetts and considers only 18thC pieces. A large sawbuck table with red wash fills the center of the Keeping Room. An assembled set of eight banister back chairs surrounds the table.

An early 18thC candle box with plain, simple lines hangs to the right of the fireplace.

Homespun blankets in soft tan tones hang from an early quilt rack.

An Indian-made burl bowl with red paint and beautiful lines rests on the table.

A stretcher base tavern table, with a single drawer to the left of the fireplace, dates to 1710. It features one huge dove tail runner in the middle of the drawer. On top, an early carved Bible Box dated 1734 holds an hour glass from the Williamsburg collection.

Shown left, an early banister back arm chair with original turnings retains its red wash.

At the end of the room, the paneled cupboard with a large molding features butterfly hinges and dates to the late 17thC. On top, a huge pantry box is constructed with a double row of nails. Hanging to the left is an early broom from a log cabin in Ohio. The handle is chip carved from an ash log; what remains from the shaved log becomes the broom. A cant-leg small Windsor stool holds a small document box and early candle stick

An early tape loom with carving on the bottom is hanging above the Queen Anne slant top desk in original red wash.

Draped on the back of the chair, an 18th wool cloak rests beneath an early hanging loom basket with original patina.

The large built-in beside the doorway leading to the kitchen is a North Shore cupboard purchased from the home's previous owner; it fits perfectly in the corner spot.

The drop leaf table in the dining room dates to the 1700's and has a tiger maple top with black painted base. It holds a burl bowl and horn cup. The banister back chairs are from Chelmsford, Massachusetts.

Four ladder back chairs in the kitchen are part of a set of ten Marge has placed throughout the house. These surround a hutch table in original red paint which features a drawer in the base. Sunlight shines on a wood bowl fashioned like a porringer on the center of the table. The painting on the back wall, painted by their son, depicts Al and Marge's garden.

A 19thC transfer ware punch bowl enjoys a place of honor on the two-drawer William and Mary lift top chest with large original ball feet.

The portrait is of New England origin, circa 1830, and is in untouched condition.

A Queen Anne style mirror in old red hangs above the Chippendale style desk made of maple and tiger maple. A diminutive lift top desk in old red paint features a scalloped interior. Standing on top is an early sander in mustard paint.

The pine cupboard in the corner with a tombstone cutout retains large original HL hinges.

The large pantry box on the bottom shelf is constructed with rose head nails and dates to the 18thC. The top shelf holds early redware. The middle shelf holds a horn cup dated 1702. A porringer and treenware on the middle shelf were pictured in Mary Earl Gould's book on woodenware.

Marge displays an early crewel pot holder on the right side of the fireplace. The small settle with old black-brown surface comes from the collection of the late and renowned New Hampshire antique dealer, Roger Bacon. The paper-mache doll dates to 1825 and is original including her clothes and red leather boots.

Marge has the provenance on the loom, dated 1728.

A small stretcher base Connecticut tea table with early turned legs and black paint is tucked in the corner to the right of the fireplace. A small six board chest with tiny feet can be seen on top. When Marge found the box, it contained a handmade little recipe book written in old script.

Standing in front of the camel back sofa in the parlor, a 1710 black gate leg table found in Massachusetts features ring and vase turnings and little ball feet.

The mirror is a William and Mary style with a nicely scrolled top. It is in untouched condition.

The maple highboy in the corner with nicely defined Queen Anne legs and bold feet is original; it features shell carving on the bottom drawers. The highboy is circa 1750.

A Hannah Davis wallpaper box, dating to the mid 19thC, is displayed on top.

The William and Mary day bed with bold turnings is probably from the Boston area, as the back shows similar design as those originating from Boston. Beneath the cushion, the day bed retains its original leather seat.

Marge was drawn to the circa 1830 untouched portrait of a young girl by the portrait's subtle colors and the sweet appearance of the sitter.

An early Connecticut 18thC lectern with original finish stands to the left of the fireplace. Above it hangs a pipe box in old black. To the right of the fireplace, a large adjustable candle holder with a "T" base stands beside a four-slat black armchair with mushroom arms.

A ladies' sewing bag with crewel can be seen hanging on the panel to the right of the fireplace. This panel is actually removable and conceals a secret area behind the front hall wall; the compartment was used to hide family members during the Revolutionary War.

The 1740 Massachusetts Queen Anne six drawer chest in old red stands in the corner of the master bedroom. The wall box on top is a Hannah Davis.

A six board chest rests at the foot of a Queen Anne low post antique bed in old red.

A Queen Anne button foot red base table with scrub top holds a little early desk in old red with handmade tin hinges. A William and Mary mirror with heart cutout retains its original glass. Below it is a framed severance receipt from a Connecticut Revolutionary soldier indicating his pay, authorized by Governor Oliver Wolcott, a signer of the Declaration of Independence.

The fireplace in the master bedroom features ten raised panels. An original Pre-Greiner doll sits in a child's settle on the hearth. The doll holds a small early tin rattle and schoolbook in her lap.

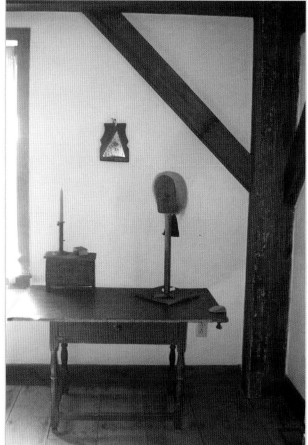

The high seven drawer chest in the guest room is valuable in that it has survived hundreds of years without pulls being added. It is made of maple and pine and holds an oval wallpaper box.

The red base tavern table in the corner has a single drawer and holds an early wig stand and small box with early carving in the front.

A fragment mirror hangs above the table; such a mirror was made from the precious fragment of a broken mirror.

Two early wall paper boxes are displayed on an early butterfly drop leaf table with splayed legs. A small Queen Anne bed with molded posts holds an old red loom.

One of the rooms upstairs is used as a weaving room. To the right of the post, a standing squirrel cage yarn winder retains its original red paint. The stick to the left of the post is a handmade yardstick. A brown homespun petticoat hangs on a peg rack on the wall.

The spinning wheel was most likely a gift to a bride from her groom as it features a delightful chip-carved heart cutout.

The early four-slat arm chair with lemon finials dates to circa 1700. Beside it is an unusual standing swift in old red. Just barely visible is an 18thC cradle used by some of the Staufer's grandchildren.

The circa 1690 chest in the corner is from Connecticut. When Marge received it from her sister-in-law, it contained an original piece of linsey-woolsey fabric and tobacco in the till. A hanging loom basket, filled with wool, hangs above.

Marge couldn't resist the six board blanket chest in the back hall- not only because she had the perfect spot for it, but because of the initials MS carved on the top.

Marge's business is called Marjorie Staufer Antiques. Her shop, located on the property, is open by chance or appointment. Marge may be reached at 330-239-1443 or by email at smarj@roadrunner.com.

Marjorie also maintains space at the Seville Antique Mall in Medina, Ohio, in addition to participating at shows during New Hampshire week. Marge also sells her fine antiques at the Heartland Antiques Show in Richmond, Indiana, and Jim Burk's York, Pennsylvania show.

My camera was unable to capture the scope of Al Staufer's model train layout in the barn encircling the loft.

Chapter 8

Mark Kimball Moulton and Lane Carpenter

Mark and Lane bought their home called Sparrow Hill in Riverton, Connecticut in 2005 and immediately began renovations to age their 21stC home to one from the 19thC. When Mark and Lane sold the Kimball Homestead, a 19thC home built by Mark's ancestors and located about a half-mile away, they intended to leave the Riverton area; they decided, though, that they couldn't leave their large circle of friends.

The house overlooks the Farmington River. Mark's background as a horticulturist and love for the outdoors inspired him to design and create a river walk. Mark often sits in this spot to generate ideas for his next children's book; he has written over 20. His first, "A Snowman Named Just Bob", published in 1999, has sold over 250,000 copies.

The raging Farmington River rushes past during the early spring thaw.

Looking into the dining room from the kitchen area, the eye is drawn to each piece of early paint with an overall splendid array of "eye candy". The farm table in early red paint is surrounded by Bentwood Windsor chairs.

The robin's egg blue wood box with slanted lift top was purchased at a local antique shop. Two manganese jugs and a crock stand on top. The early basket hides the thermostat.

An early 19thC cupboard with missing door on the bottom simply means more display space for crocks, manganese pottery, stoneware, and redware. Tucked in the corner on the bottom is an apple green painted firkin. Two early birdhouses and a blue painted basket rest on top.

A mustard bowl rack holds an array of dough bowls with paint and early attic surface. Beneath is a pumpkin painted jelly cupboard holding redware. The black and red game board is Canadian, identified by the number of squares. A blue-green corner cupboard found at Brimfield, Massachusetts can be seen through the chandelier.

A collection of hand crafted animals, done by Kay Cloud, fill a small wall shelf here and across the room.

An old red ladder holds a collection of baskets. Mark has covered the Formica counters he and Lane inherited with early cutting boards. Two large tin lidded early apothecary jars can be seen under a large pear painting and a 19thC grater. The corner sink is a black composition sink purchased at Home Depot.

Mark and Lane stacked two early painted cupboards in the kitchen and use it as a pantry. The blue cupboard in the area off the kitchen is probably Canadian and was purchased at the Buggy Whip Factory in western Massachusetts.

Two early barn lanterns hang in the corner of the living room. Folded blankets and coverlets are stacked on top of a large bookcase beside an early splint. A Pennsylvania old grain scoop hangs on the side of the bookcase. The coffee table is a stretcher base early table with small drawer and early green paint.

Early books, a folksy arrow weathervane, and some of Lane's collection of early dogs are shown on shelves over the couch.

A small remnant of metal hearts from a larger mat creates a nice pattern on the wall.

Over the mantel, three early pastoral landscapes form a backdrop for a collection of hogscrapers and leather bound books.

A fabulous 19thC dry painted red six board chest with boot jack ends holds two early unglazed crocks.

The small watercolor portrait depicts Mark's great-great-great grandfather.

The cozy side porch features lots of early baskets suspended from beams, wicker furniture, and a scrub top table with dry black paint. Mark bought the set of four chairs at a flea market for $80.

I love what Mark and Lane did in the first floor bathroom. Using an old window frame with attached shutters in original blue paint, they replaced the window panes with a mirror.

Mark maintains a website www.markkimballmoulton.com where information on his books and schedule is available.

Chapter 9

Kathy and Dick Hopper

Kathy, a retired nurse, now owns *Early Birds Estate Sales* on Cape Cod, which brings her in contact with resources for antiques. Kathy and her husband Dick, a retired real estate broker, bought their cape in 1994. The house, built in the 1970's on a heavily wooded lot, features stucco walls throughout and wide-board New England pine floors.

Kathy painted the living room trim paint with an Old Village paint called "Pearwood".

Early pewter chargers with wonderful patina rest on the mantel on either side of a framed print called Westward Ho.

The center of the mantel holds a metal box with handles which is actually a French fish poacher.

An early salt glazed stoneware butter churn is seen on the hearth.

The desk to the right of the fireplace is an early pine schoolmaster's desk with original porcelain knobs. When Kathy found the piece, she was shopping with a woman who remarked, "You're not really going to put that piece of junk in your house?"

A 19thC dry sink holds baskets, crocks, an early dough bowl, and a small spice chest in the well. The basket on top called a Higgins basket was made in Chesterfield, New York, circa 1900.

Kathy has filled a 19thC blue painted tool carrier with rag balls made from early homespun. Dick and Kathy bought the maple drop leaf table at an auction on the Cape.

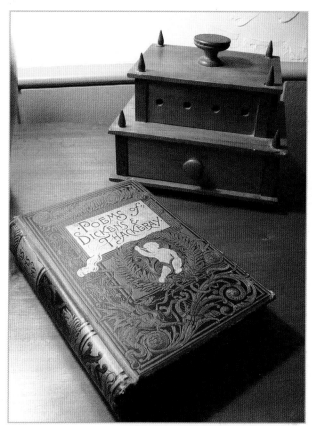

A Shaker sewing box rests on the 19thC single drawer table. The sampler above the table was wrought in 1819 by Volina Cary, a seventh-generation descendant of John Alden and Priscilla Mullins.

The four-slat ladder back chair is early and has shortened arms purportedly to accommodate the large hoop skirts worn in the 18thC.

A wide single board bench holds a carrier with chrome yellow paint and a delightful heart cutout. A small slide top candle box can be seen alongside.

Kathy displays ovoid salt-glazed jugs and stoneware crocks on a bench in front of the seldom-used front door.

The cupboard alongside the stairway features a single-board door. A reproduction spoon rack hangs above.

Kathy has filled the tall corner cupboard with some of her collection of blue and white pottery and white ironstone. The Windsor bentwood chair is early and pegged throughout.

A single-board top table in the family room is tucked beside the couch and holds
a six drawer cubby.

The working clocks are both early. The clock over the mustard jelly cupboard is an old Regulator school clock dating to the late 19thC.

Kathy displays early scrub boards on the wall of the downstairs bathroom. An old wooden lantern with a tin back hangs from a peg on the back wall.

A primitive bench holds a bail-handled pantry box with red pip berries.

An apothecary with white paint sits at the end of the mantel and holds a decoy dating to the late 19thC. The sampler over the mantel is 19thC.

The pine stepback cupboard dates to the 19thC; the previous owners cut the cupboard into two pieces to accommodate their low ceilings.

A 19thC blue and white quilt is folded on top of the family-room couch.

A small cupboard holds small early baskets, a pewter mug, and a painted decoy.

Kathy has a passion for apothecary chests and has tastefully placed them throughout the house.

The tole-painted tray is early; Kathy was drawn to the composition and detail of the work. Unfortunately she has little information on the artist.

The dining room table is a 19thC hutch table with two drawers. It has a pegged top and holds a large trencher filled with cranberries.

Kathy has lined the top shelf of the pewter cupboard with her collection of graduated small berry baskets.

A standing dough box nestles in the corner beside another apothecary in dry chalky gray white paint.

An interesting candle box with terrific patina, perhaps a make-do, holds a newly crafted doll.

The home's previous owners installed the antique mantel in the dining room which Kathy uses to display more early miniature baskets and a small two-drawer pine spice chest.

The apothecary atop the early gray bench is probably the earliest Kathy owns. The porcelain knobs are original to the piece.

Beneath the double window, a long bench holds a row of stoneware crocks. The shorebird on the window sill is unusual in that it is made of tin rather than carved from wood.

Kathy has covered her kitchen counters with cutting boards. A small chest to the right of the sink holds drinking cups.

A vintage Barrus mustard tin rests on the counter beside an early tin-lidded apothecary jar.

Kathy was told the handled jug on top of the small spice chest is an oyster pot. A candle box which Kathy uses to hold early treen kitchen utensils has a wonderful heart etched on the front.

A matched set of bird cage Windsor chairs surrounds the oxblood 19thC table. A tin dough board and rolling pin are seen hanging on the wall in the corner.

A small stool holds a double-sided tin spice box atop the early pie safe.

Kathy's pantry is chock full of early treasures: yellow ware bowls, molds, jars, measures, pantry boxes, and butter presses, to name a few. Shown top left, an English plate rack holds early pewter plates.

Kathy had the pantry designed to accommodate the large apothecary seen above right.

A large beehive dough bowl in red paint hangs on the pantry wall above a board with heart cutout.

Kathy isn't sure what the tin piece hanging above the standing butter churn in mustard paint was used for, but was drawn to the piece for its patina and unusual shape.

On the upstairs landing, what looks to be an apothecary is actually an early shoe maker's cupboard.

Kathy has hung early brushes on the leather strap where the shoemaker's brushes would have been stored.

The hooked rug hanging in the landing and shown left blends beautifully with the tones of the shoemaker's cabinet.

Early pharmaceutical mortar and pestles rest on top of the apothecary in the master bathroom. The small four-drawer chest above it is made of tin.

A shelf above the commode holds early apothecary jars, a lidded tin container, and a small creamy white bail handled pantry box.

Kathy has found the perfect spot for the small cheese safe with original screens.

Kathy found the vintage quilt at an estate sale. The twig star above the bed ties in nicely with the pattern on the quilt. The chest of drawers beside the bed is a Hitchcock piece.

A walnut marble top commode is angled in the corner and holds a tole-painted small document box.

Kathy uses an early trundle bed as a spare bed for grandchildren.

Kathy maintains a website for Early Bird Estate Sales, *www.earlybirdsestatesales.com*, and may also be reached via her email *kathyhopper@comcast.net*.

Because it takes almost two years between the time I photograph homes and the finished book arrives, I generally work on multiple books at a time. I'm excited about the books I have planned for 2011.

Following *The Country Life, Simply Country Gardens*, created during the dead of winter, will be available in February at a time when we are dreaming of spring and the beauty of flowers.

In May, *The Spirit of Country* will continue the house tour format and capture the homes of families in Connecticut, Massachusetts, Maine, New Hampshire and Indiana.

The *Joy of Country* will be available in July and include homes in Pennsylvania, Virginia, Connecticut, Massachusetts, New York and West Virginia. One home featured will be that of renowned folk artist Christopher Gurshin and his wife Janice.

Holidays at a Country Home will capture the holiday spirit with hundreds of pictures showing how we use our country home as a fresh palette during that warm and welcoming time of the year. This all holiday book will be available in September.

The final book in 2011, *A Touch of Country* is planned for release in the late fall.

I continue to look forward to finding new homes to photograph, more ideas to share, and the opportunity to meet new friends. I am currently photographing homes for 2012 and will continue the "simply country" books as long as my loyal readers ask for them.

The "simply country" book series
by Judy Condon

Country on a Shoestring

Of Hearth and Home

A Simpler Time

Country Decorating for All Seasons
- holiday doors, porches, mantels, trees, vignettes; summer gardens, and fall decorating

As Time Goes By

Country at Heart
- The Tavern Room; early looms, dolls and bears; The Gathering Room; a kitchen aged to perfection; country gardens

Welcome Home
- New house tour format; 2 Connecticut homes and 5 Ohio Homes; plus a never before photographed Shaker collection

Home Again
- 7 Ohio homes, 1 Maine home

The Warmth of Home
- 3 Massachusetts homes, 1 Pennsylvania home, 3 Ohio homes, 1 New York home and 1 Delaware home

The Country Home
- 6 Ohio homes, 2 Massachusetts homes, 1 New Hampshire home

The Comfort of Home
- Over 325 color photographs showing a Massachusetts and Ohio home of two exceptional collectors. A Maine home; three Massachusetts homes, one of which is in the city; a New Hampshire home decorated in "first period".

Simple Greens - Simply Country
- An all holiday book. Over 400 color photographs showing homes decorated "simply" with greenery for the holiday season.